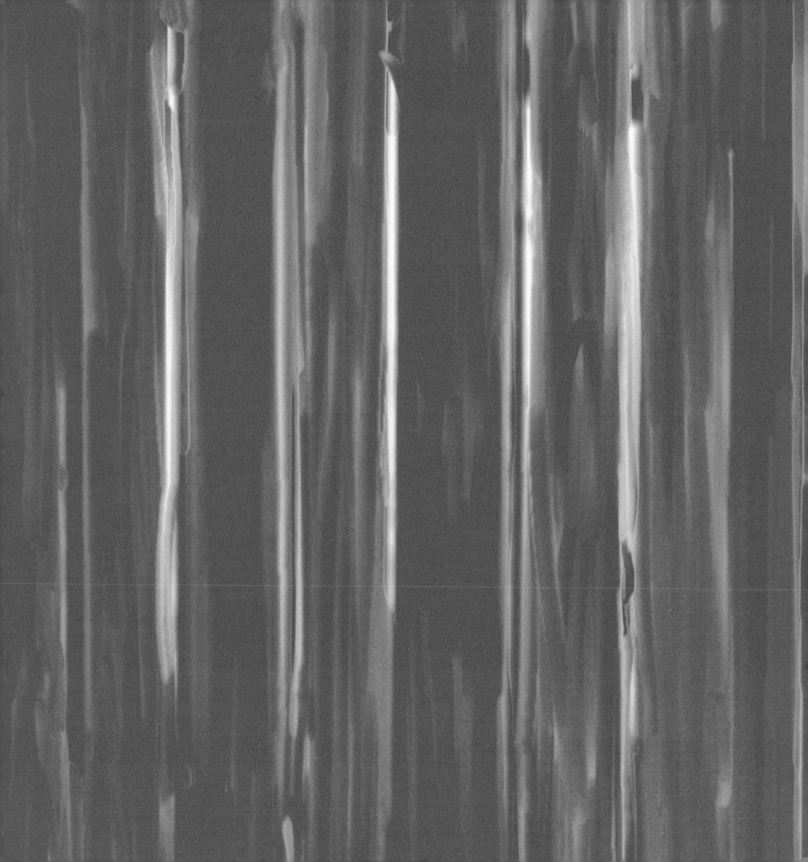

Dedicated to the children who are waiting
and the parents who are longing.

Copyright © 2012 by Christina Kyllonen and Peter Greer

All rights reserved. No portion of this book may be reproduced, stored in a retrieval system, or transmitted in any form or by any means—electronic, mechanical, photocopy, recording, scanning, or other—except for brief quotations in critical reviews or articles, without the prior written permission of the authors.

A publication of 4-more | Lancaster, Pennsylvania

4-more is a 501(c)(3) non-profit organization that partners with Rwandan communities to develop sustainable clean water, sanitation and health initiatives. 4-more also provides adoption support through the rubymyles fund. Learn more at www.4-more.org.

ISBN: 978-1-937498-06-1

Publication, distribution and fulfillment services provided by Russell Media (Boise, ID). www.russell-media.com

This book may be purchased in bulk for educational, business, or promotional use.

For information, please email info@4-more.org.

Cover design, illustrations, and layout by Jeff Brown. www.browndesigner.com

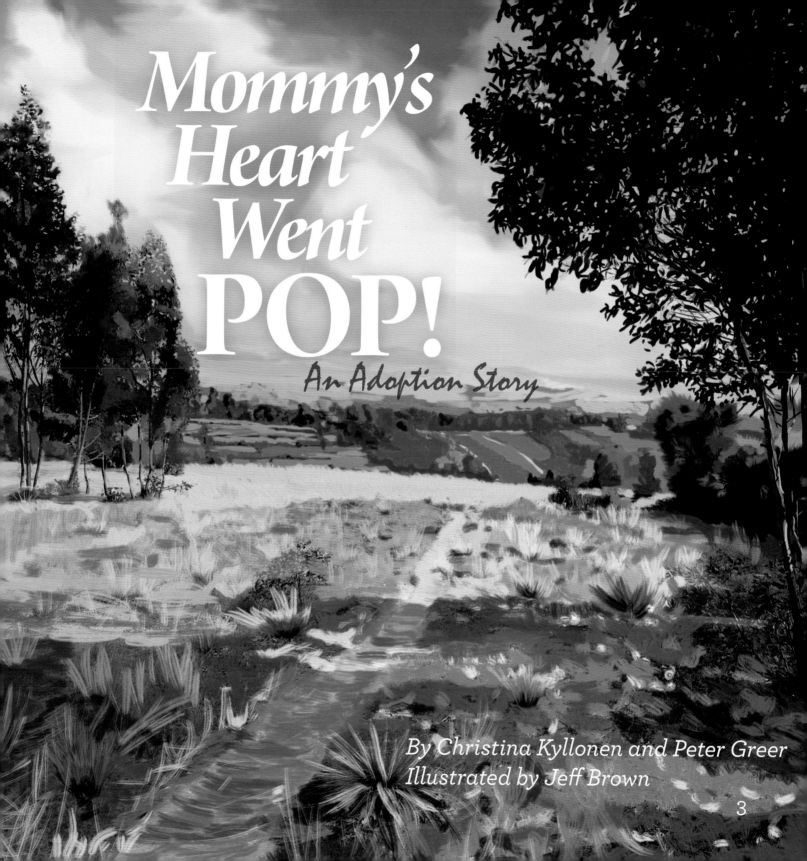

Mommy's Heart Went POP!

An Adoption Story

By Christina Kyllonen and Peter Greer
Illustrated by Jeff Brown

3

One night in the land of rolling hills, hot sun and mosquito nets, a tiny bundle all wrapped up in blankets was carefully placed in front of a bright blue door.

The door opened and a tall woman with kind eyes poked her head out and looked around. When she saw you wrapped up in blankets and sleeping soundly, she scooped you up into her arms and carried you inside.

5

Far away, on the other side of the world,
a mommy was dreaming of a baby with
round eyes the color of chocolate.
The mommy already had two children,
but knew there was room for more.

6

She explained to them that she had a baby growing in her heart, not in her belly like so many other mommies.

7

Each day as the mommy combed
her little girl's hair, she wondered
who was combing your hair.

8

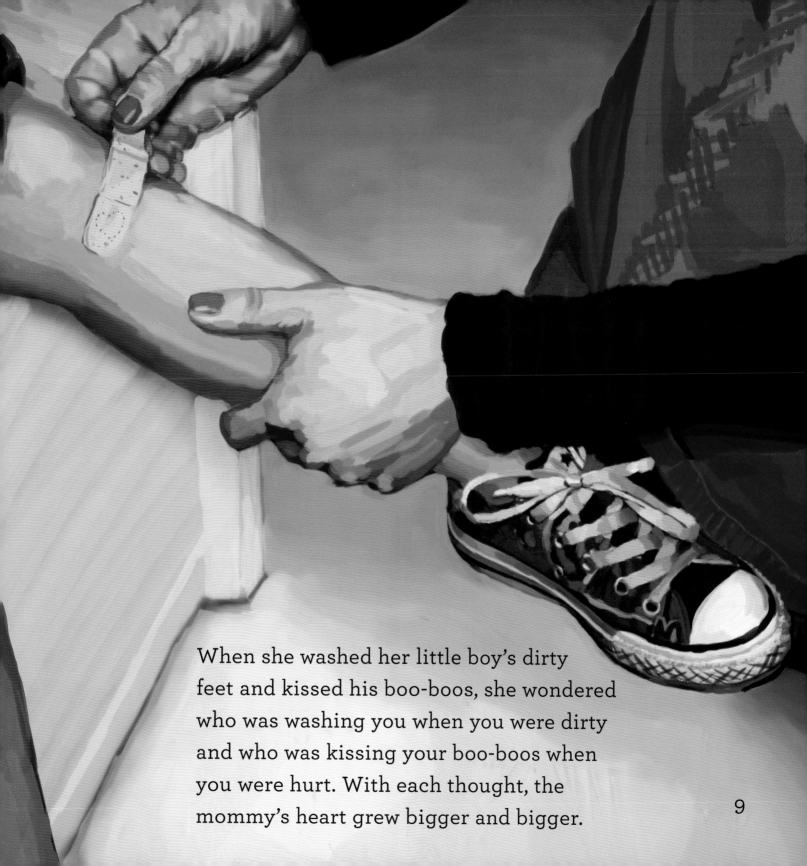

When she washed her little boy's dirty feet and kissed his boo-boos, she wondered who was washing you when you were dirty and who was kissing your boo-boos when you were hurt. With each thought, the mommy's heart grew bigger and bigger.

9

At night when she tucked the little boy and little girl into bed, she would sing them a lullaby. As she sang, she wondered if somebody was whispering a lullaby into your ear, and her heart grew a little bit bigger.

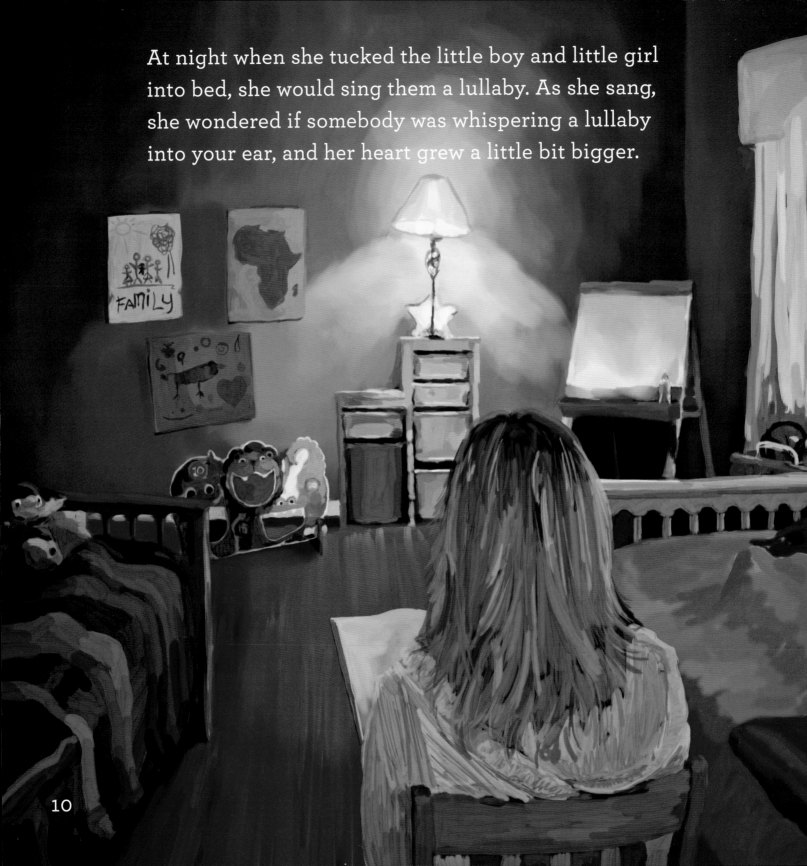

Late at night she would lay in bed and dream of you. She wondered what you looked like and how it would feel to snuggle you close to her. And because she could do nothing else, she prayed that you were being loved while you waited for her. Her heart grew bigger still.

As days and weeks
and months passed,

the mommy's heart kept
getting bigger and bigger.

12

Sometimes it felt
so big, in fact,

that it even hurt!

14

The mommy kept busy getting ready
for you to come home. She painted
a room for you and bought clothes
that would fit you just right.

Friends who knew how big
your mommy's heart was
getting even had a party to
celebrate that one day soon
you would come home.

They ate cake and opened
presents that were just for you.

17

That night the mommy sat in the room that was waiting for you too.

She closed her eyes so that she could picture you in it, and her heart grew just a bit bigger.

One starry night,
after the little boy
and little girl had
been put to bed, the
phone rang. The
voice on the other
end said that it was
finally time to go.

The mommy and daddy were so excited!

They jumped on an airplane that flew through the clouds to take them to the other side of the world to the land of rolling hills, hot sun and mosquito nets—the place where you were waiting.

Before they
knew it, they
were walking
through
a bright
blue door.

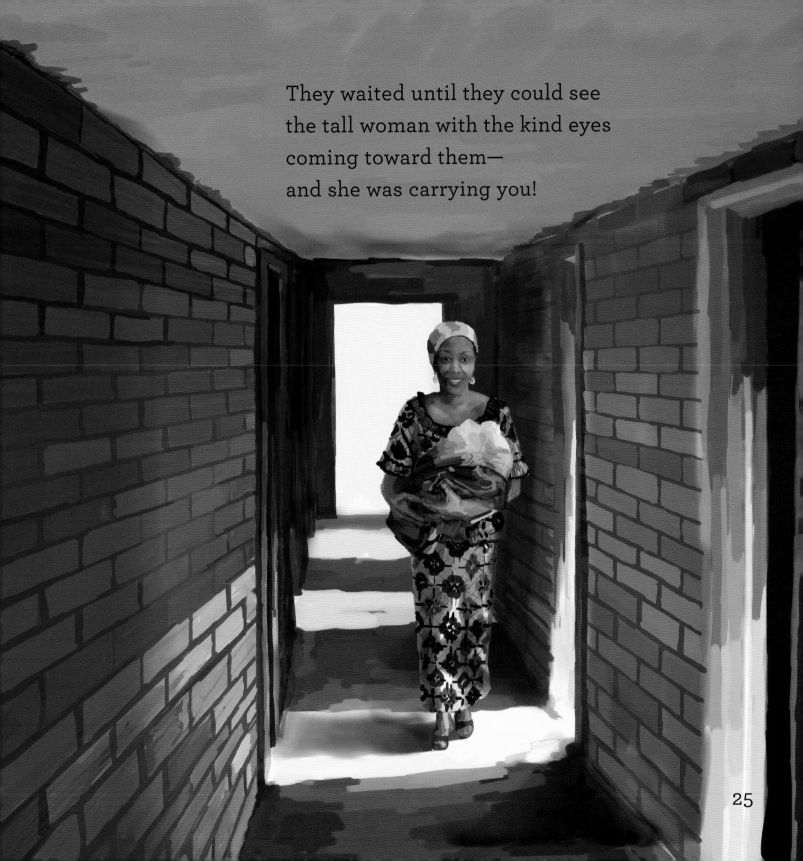

They waited until they could see
the tall woman with the kind eyes
coming toward them—
and she was carrying you!

25

The woman smiled and
handed you to your mommy,
and it was on that day,
at that very moment,
that your mommy's
great big heart went POP!
And all of the love that she
had been saving just for you
came pouring out.

Your mommy looked deep into your big round eyes. She kissed the tip of your little nose. She counted ten little fingers and ten little toes and she whispered a lullaby into your ear. And then she did what she had been waiting to do for so long...

she took you home.

Afterword

Both of our families had our hearts "pop" when we decided to walk through our own blue doors. We welcomed our adopted children into our arms and into our hearts. When we hear our children laugh, see their dimples and wipe away their tears, we thank God for bringing our precious children home.

But as we walked away from the orphanage, we couldn't walk away from the many children who were still waiting for their families. They are among the millions of other children longing to call someone mommy and daddy.

We encourage you to consider how your family can get involved.

For some, you recognize you have room in your heart and in your home to adopt a child. Resources include:

ABBA FUND
www.abbafund.org

BETHANY CHRISTIAN SERVICES
www.bethany.org

AMERICA WORLD ADOPTION
www.awaa.org

GLADNEY CENTER FOR ADOPTION
www.adoptionsbygladney.com

As life-changing as international adoption can be, it will never be enough to solve the global orphan crisis. We believe that local solutions are often the most powerful ways to provide for children. Organizations we believe are effectively acting to address the global orphan crisis include:

4-MORE
www.4-more.org

COMPASSION INTERNATIONAL
www.compassion.com

AFRICA NEW LIFE MINISTRIES
www.africanewlife.org

HOPE INTERNATIONAL
www.hopeinternational.org

CHILDREN'S HOPE CHEST
www.hopechest.org

LIFESONG FOR ORPHANS
www.lifesongfororphans.org

May your heart continue to grow until each child has a home.

Christina and Peter

Acknowledgments

This book would not have happened without the love and support of our family and friends who supported us each step of our journeys. Special thanks to Chad Kyllonen, Laurel Greer, Allison Brown, Alanna Heath and Heather Hohenwarter. Additional support and encouragement came from the Board of HOPE International, partners at Clapham Capital, Becky Svendsen, Angela Scheff, Anna Haggard, Scott Todd, Karen Yates, Jason Locy, Mark Russell, John and Sharna Coors, Christine Baingana and Sarah Sparling.

About the Authors

CHRISTINA KYLLONEN is a co-founder of 4-more, a 501(c)(3) non-profit organization that partners with Rwandan communities to develop sustainable clean water, sanitation and health initiatives. 4-more also provides adoption support through the rubymyles fund. Christina and her husband, Chad, have four children and chronicle their adoption journey at *adoptingruby.blogspot.com*. They live in Elizabethtown, PA.

PETER GREER is the president of HOPE International, a Christ-centered organization combatting extreme poverty in Africa, Asia, the Caribbean and Eastern Europe. He is co-author of *The Poor Will Be Glad* and blogs at *www.peterkgreer.com*. Peter and his wife, Laurel, have three children and share their adoption story at *milestomyles.blogspot.com*. They live in Lancaster, PA.

JEFF BROWN is a full time designer for HOPE International and a freelance designer at *www.browndesigner.com*. He lives with his wife, Allison, and their two children in Lancaster, PA.

All the proceeds of this book will go to the "rubymyles fund." This fund is administered by 4-more and provides grants for adoption and support to organizations addressing the orphan crisis.

www.4-more.org

With your child, find the hidden heart in each picture.

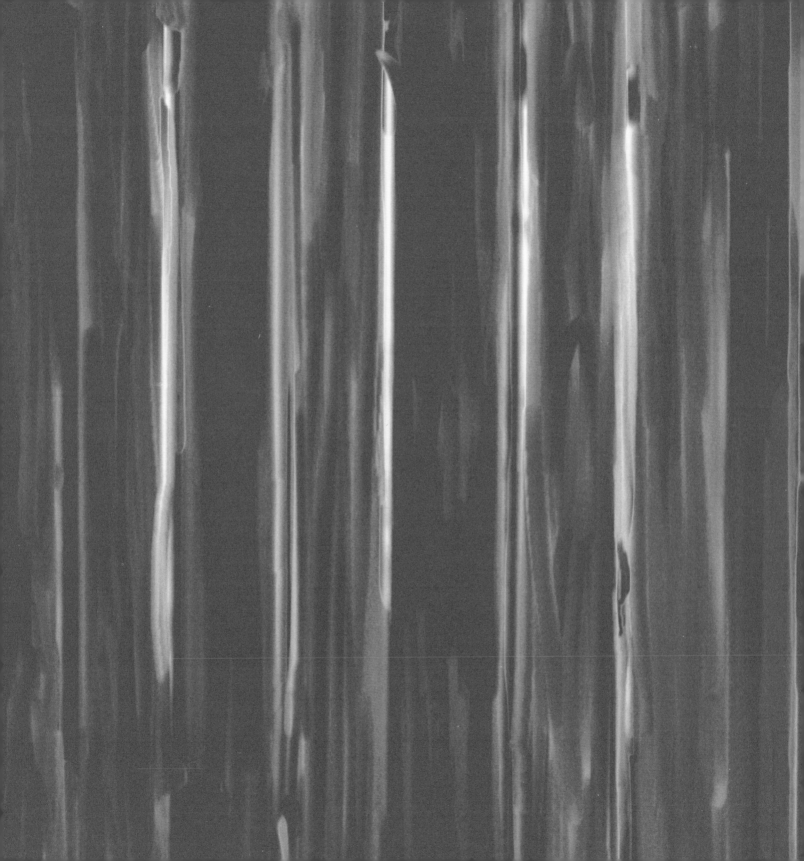